INVENTORS & INVENTIONS

VIDEO

INVENTORS & INVENTIONS
VIDEO

JACKIE BIEL

BENCHMARK BOOKS

MARSHALL CAVENDISH
NEW YORK

Benchmark Books
Marshall Cavendish Corporation
99 White Plains Road
Tarrytown, New York 10591-9001

©Marshall Cavendish Corporation, 1996

Series created by The Creative Publishing Company

Library of Congress Cataloging-in-Publication Data

Biel, Jackie.
    Video / Jackie Biel.
       p.   cm. -- (Inventors & inventions)
    Includes index.
    Summary: Discusses the development of video technology, some of
its current uses for entertainment, education, and business, as well
as future possibilities.
    ISBN 0-7614-0048-6 (lib. bdg.)
    1. Television--Juvenile literature.   2. Video recording--Juvenile
literature.   3. Video recordings--Social aspects--Juvenile
literature.   [1. Video recording.   2. Television.]   I. Title.
II. Series.
TK6640.B53   1996
621.388--dc20
                                       95-41573
                                         CIP
                                       AC

Printed in Hong Kong

Acknowledgments

Technical Consultant: Teodoro C. Robles, Ph.D.
Illustrations on pages 16, 18, 19, and 22 by Julian Baker

The publishers would like to thank the following for their permission to reproduce photographs:
Ampex Corporation, (10, 11, 12, 13, 14, 15); Associated Press/Topham, (47); Eye Ubiquitous, (36, 41, 53, Tim Page 25, Gavin Wickham 42); Museum of the Moving Image, (51); Science Photo Library Ltd., (James King-Holmes front cover, Gontier 7, Philippe Plailly 20, Takeshi Takahara 23, Peter Menzel 28, David Guyon 35, James King-Holmes 39, Hank Morgan 40, Philippe Plailly 44, John Greim 45, NASA 46, Peter Menzel 55, Hank Morgan 58, David Parker 59); Sony, (30, 32, 33); Tony Stone Images, (frontispiece, 37, 43, 54); Topham Picture Point (48); UPI/Bettmann (8, 31).

(Cover) A video screen in the cockpit of a flight simulator imitates the approach to Hong Kong airport at dusk.

(Frontispiece) Business executives take part in a video conference.

Contents

— Chapter 1 —
A Vision Called Video

A shadowy figure slips quietly along a dark alley. Its shoes make no sound; the face is almost hidden under a soft slouch hat. A thin cat scuttles out of the way as the figure approaches a small doorway and knocks softly. After a few tense seconds, the door opens, money changes hands, and the figure runs silently away.

A few minutes later, three unmarked police cars with their headlights off glide quietly into the alley and stop. Police officers surround the dark doorway, their guns drawn and ready. There is a knock, the door opens, a light suddenly glares, a scuffle, and a drug dealer is subdued and led away in handcuffs.

In court, the dealer is tried and convicted. The evidence is a videotape taken by a video camera little bigger than a quarter concealed in the headband of the informant's slouch hat. The tiny camera had recorded the entire drug transaction.

This fictional scene would not have been possible fifty years ago, before video became a workable technology. Now, tiny transmitters and miniature video cameras that record pictures even in the dark help police and security forces in their work.

Video Is Everywhere

Video, in the form of television broadcasting and cable, has become one of the world's major sources of information and entertainment since it was first developed almost three-quarters of a century ago. Broadcast and cable television bring moving pictures and sound into hundreds of millions of homes around the world, taking the place of newspapers, magazines, and books as the most popular information and entertainment source for most people. In fact, when the videocassette recorder started to become standard equipment in the home, even movie theaters had to radically change their businesses just to survive.

But although it is most evident there, video is not used just in the home. Forms of video technology, from the simplest to the most sophisticated, have become practically indispensable in almost all areas of modern human endeavor. Schools, businesses, hospitals, research institutions, and many other organizations use video for every purpose imaginable — from creating colorful images of atoms to bringing breathtaking pictures of faraway galaxies to Earth. And with the dawning in the 1990s of what sociologists call the information age, computers and video have

A Japanese man uses a home videophone. In only a few years, video technology has entered homes across the world and become a part of everyday life.

combined to bring the resources of libraries, museums, and art galleries all over the world to anyone at the touch of a keyboard.

How It All Started

In the late 1800s, Guglielmo Marconi discovered that electromagnetic waves could carry signals through the air at the speed of light. These waves are generated by the oscillation (the movement back and forth) of electric charges, such as electrons. Soon, people figured out how to turn sounds into electromagnetic waves, transmit them over distance, and then turn them back into sounds with a radio receiver at the other end.

From there, it was possible to imagine sending pictures through the air as well. In 1922, Philo T. Farnsworth, a U.S. scientist, developed a way to scan pictures electronically, turning them into electromagnetic impulses that could be sent over distances. But his pictures were blurry and jittery, almost unrecognizable. The next year, a Russian-born American named Vladimir K. Zworykin invented the iconoscope and the kinescope. The iconoscope was the first device to make recognizable television pictures. The kinescope was a prototype of the modern television picture tube, the very first TV receiver.

During the next twenty years, engineers developed better and better transmitters and receivers. By the mid-1940s, television was popular all over the United States. This gave rise to a new multibillion dollar industry of TV networks, program producers, and thousands of advertising agencies to prepare and sell the TV commercials that supported the new industry.

The style of television and radio in the home in 1947, twenty-five years after the invention of the technology that made TV possible. By 1955, most U.S. homes had a television set.

The German Secret

Meanwhile, radio had been rapidly growing, and hundreds of radio programs were on the air. But everything had to be aired live — there was no way to record programs for later broadcast.

During World War II, a U.S. Army engineer named Jack Mullin found a device called a Magnetophon in a radio studio in Germany. This machine used plastic tape coated with iron oxide particles to record sound. Mullin secretly disassembled two Magnetophons and mailed them home to the U.S., where he later reassembled them. Suddenly, here was what everyone had been waiting for — a way to record audio for broadcast later.

Soon, people started thinking about recording video. But video was much harder to put on tape than audio; there was so much more electronic information to record that miles of video-tape would have to pass over the recording heads at about thirty-three feet (ten meters) per second in order to produce even one video program. Clearly, unless the system was redesigned altogether, video recording would be impossible.

The problem intrigued an engineer named Marvin Camras. He mounted the recording heads on a rotating drum and attached the drum to a vacuum cleaner motor. This increased the relative speed of the tape over the heads so it could record the video signals.

Engineers from Ampex saw Camras's rotating-head videotape recorder. Ampex was a small California electronics firm founded in 1944 by a Russian immigrant named Alexander M. Poniatoff. His engineers were excited about Camras's recorder and told Poniatoff about it. The new television industry was having the same problem that the radio industry had had — everything had to be aired live, and people were looking for a cheaper way to broadcast the programs. The Ampex engineers thought the rotating-head recorder just might be the answer. Poniatoff liked the idea, too, so in January 1952, he hired an electrical engineer named Charles Pauson Ginsburg to head the new project.

AMAZING FACTS

The first public demonstration of television recorded on magnetic tape was made on November 11, 1951. Jack Mullin and Wayne Johnson, another radio engineer, recorded airplanes taking off and landing by using standard 1/4-inch audio tape, running past the heads at 360 inches (9.1 meters) per second. The picture was so poor that Mullin said if they hadn't provided a running commentary, the audience wouldn't have known what they were looking at.

Charles Ginsburg (1920–1992)

Charles Pauson Ginsburg was born July 27, 1920, and grew up in California. As a boy, he was fascinated with electronics and once nearly electrocuted himself building a crystal radio set. But he was most intrigued by a new technology called television. After graduating from San Jose State in 1948 with a major in mathematics and engineering, he looked for work in television, but the closest he could get was a night job operating the transmitter at a San Jose radio station.

Then fate intervened. Alexander M. Poniatoff, founder and president of Ampex, was looking for someone to design a video recorder for television broadcast stations. He thought the job would be almost impossible, and he wanted someone young and naive enough to believe it could be done anyway. So when one of Ginsburg's neighbors introduced the two, Poniatoff offered him the job. Ginsburg, then only thirty-one years old, jumped at the chance.

In January 1952, Ginsburg began work on the video recorder. A part-time Ampex employee named Ray Dolby heard about the "secret" project and convinced Ginsburg to let him help. Seven months later, the two had developed a black-and-white video recorder. The pictures were extremely snowy, but the machine worked well enough to warrant further development.

By August 1953, Ginsburg had recruited four more engineers for the project, and in 1955, Dolby, who had spent almost two years in the army, rejoined the team. Like any group of people, the engineers sometimes had trouble getting along with each other. But everyone liked Ginsburg. He was always cheerful, and he laughed at everyone's jokes, no matter how bad they were. Maybe, says one historian, his good spirits were a result of the diabetes he had suffered from since childhood. He was one of the first people in the world to be treated with insulin, and he felt lucky to be alive.

By March 1955, the six engineers had developed the Mark I Quad video recorder. The machine was good enough that they decided to unveil it at a meeting of television executives in Chicago the next year. Two months before the Chicago meeting, Ginsburg and his engineers went into high gear, practically living at the Ampex labs. But the result was worth it. The final product, the Mark IV Quad, produced almost perfect pictures.

It was a dramatic unveiling. An executive from CBS made an opening speech with a live image playing on several black-and-white TV monitors in the room. Then, the speaker stepped aside, and the monitors began to replay his speech. The unsuspecting audience stared in astonishment at the screens. Suddenly, curtains behind the podium parted to reveal an elegant machine in a polished steel and wood console. It was the first truly broadcast quality videotape recorder ever made.

Ginsburg continued to work for Ampex until he retired in 1986 as the company's vice president for advanced development. Among the many awards he received for his work were the David Sarnoff Gold Medal from the Society of Motion Picture and Television Engineers and the Vladimir K. Zworykin Television Prize from the Institute of Radio Engineers. After he retired, Ginsburg lived in Eugene, Oregon, until his death on April 9, 1992.

"CBS Evening News" makes the first recorded news broadcast from Los Angeles.

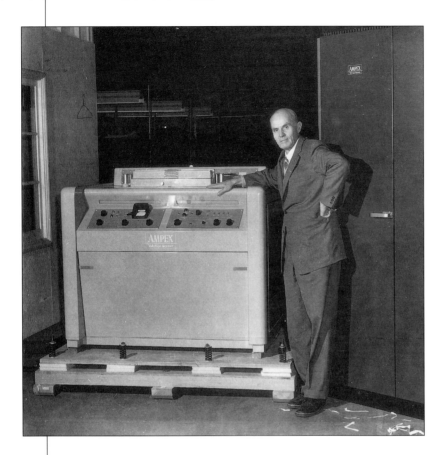

Alexander Poniatoff, the founder of Ampex, with the VR-1000, the production model of the first successful videotape recorder. The large cabinet behind him holds all the electronic equipment needed to operate the machine.

A Persistent Teenager

The video recorder project was top-secret, but somehow a nineteen-year-old college student by the name of Ray Dolby heard about it and started to pester Ginsburg unmercifully. That summer, Ginsburg finally gave in and let Dolby look at the new television recorder.

Dolby had been working part-time at Ampex since his high school years. Now, he began tinkering with the television recorder in his spare time. By November 1952, Ginsburg and Dolby were able to record a videotape of a cowboy show. But when they played it back for Poniatoff, the picture was so blurry that Poniatoff had to ask which figure was the horse and which was the cowboy!

A few weeks later, after more improvements, Ginsburg and Dolby recorded a *Krazy Kat* cartoon. And by March 1953, they had figured out how to eliminate the last of their problems — horizontal streaks caused by the crossover from one rotating recording head to the next.

It was just in time. In summer of 1953, Dolby was drafted into the U.S. Army.

Everybody on the Bandwagon

Meanwhile, RCA, a company that made radio and television equipment, was busy trying to come up with its own recorder. David Sarnoff, the head of RCA and founder of the NBC television network, had asked his research department to develop a video recorder. The system, called Simplex, was demonstrated to the public in December 1953. One machine recorded color pictures, and another recorded black-and-white. It took about a mile of ¹/₂-inch videotape to record four minutes of color pictures.

Back at Ampex, Ginsburg and a team of engineers continued to work on the video recorder project. There were many, many hurdles to overcome, but the team kept on working, sometimes putting in one hundred hours a week or more. Finally, in 1956, the very first commercial black-and-white video recorder was ready. It was a huge machine, the size of a desk, and it took two people to run it. But the videotape recorder (VTR) recorded perfect pictures. When it was demonstrated at a meeting of television station owners in Chicago, the executives broke out in wild applause. And in just four days, Ampex took in five million dollars in orders for the new videotape recorder.

AMAZING FACTS

Although the newspaper reporters invited to the RCA demonstration were impressed, there were rumors that Sarnoff had taken out the first ten rows of theater seats. That way no one could sit close enough to the TV screens to notice the poor picture quality!

TV executives meeting in Chicago in 1956 are shown the Ampex VTR. With near perfect pictures, videotape recordings had finally reached the standard required to prerecord TV programs.

Ray Dolby

Ray Milton Dolby was fascinated with physics even before he started school. At six years, he was building simple machines with parts he found in his home. Then, he started building models of soapbox racers and small engines. When he was thirteen, he built his very own motorcycle with a two-thirds horsepower engine.

Dolby's family lived in Palo Alto, California, a community near San Francisco. In junior high, his interests switched to electronics, and in high school, he joined the film projection crew. One day, Alexander Poniatoff called to ask if one of the students could show a film to a local health society. The pay was five dollars and dinner. Ray Dolby was available.

Poniatoff, founder and president of Ampex, was always on the lookout for talented people. He liked the teenager and took him to the company's labs to see a new audio recorder that the engineers had just built. It was February 1949.

That summer, Poniatoff invited Dolby to work at Ampex. Before they met him, the other engineers were skeptical about the teenager's abilities. But Poniatoff hired Dolby to make calibrated audiotapes to measure and regulate the amplification and volume of Ampex's audio recorders.

Dolby worked part-time at Ampex all through his senior year in high school and his first year at college. He developed an electronic method for controlling the speed and position of audiotape as it passed the recording heads; this would prove important later when he started working on Ampex's video recorder.

About this time, Charles Ginsburg joined Ampex to lead the new video project, and Dolby began working with him. The first problem was to slow down the speed at which the videotape had to pass the recording heads. So Dolby devised a rotating drum to hold the recording heads. Because the drum rotated, the tape itself could move more slowly. The picture was extremely blurry, recalls Dolby, but it was recognizable.

In 1953, Dolby was drafted into the U.S. Army, where he taught electronics to young recruits. Afterward, he returned to California where he entered Stanford University and rejoined Ampex. It was Dolby, still in his early twenties, who designed the final electronics for the world's first commercially successful videotape recorder.

After graduating from Stanford with a degree in electrical engineering, Dolby went to England to study at Cambridge University where he earned a Ph.D. in physics. A few years later, he opened his own engineering laboratory in London. He also met and married a young woman named Dagmar Baumert with whom he had two sons. By 1977, the family had moved to San Francisco where Dolby started another branch of his company.

A blurred video image captured from a TV screen by an early, experimental version of Ampex's VTR.

Ray Dolby is most famous for his Dolby sound system, which reduces tape hiss and other interfering noise from audio recordings. He has won many awards for his work on videotape and sound systems, including an Oscar, two Emmys, and a Grammy. He also was made an Officer of the Order of the British Empire by Queen Elizabeth II.

He now lives and works in San Francisco with his wife and two yellow Labrador dogs. For relaxation, Dolby attends the opera or flies his TBM 700 single-engine turboprop airplane.

Chapter 2
How Video Works

The video camera is made up of a lens, a pickup device, and a system of electronic circuits. The lens gathers light reflected from objects. Then, it focuses the light on the pickup device, which changes the light energy into electronic impulses. The

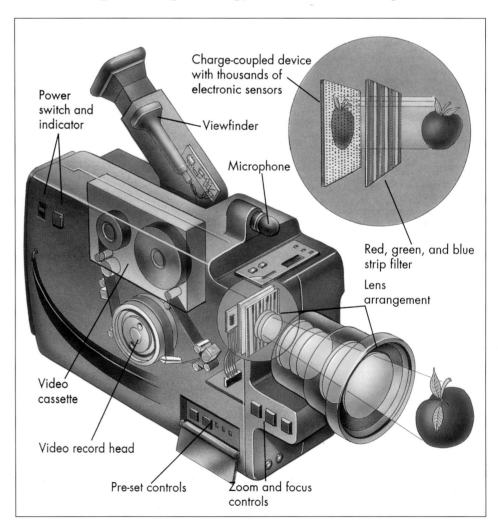

Light entering the lens of a modern three-chip video camera is broken up into its three primary colors and changed into separate electronic signals before being recorded on videotape.

Power switch and indicator

Viewfinder

Charge-coupled device with thousands of electronic sensors

Microphone

Red, green, and blue strip filter

Lens arrangement

Video cassette

Video record head

Pre-set controls

Zoom and focus controls

electronic impulses can then be recorded by a videotape recorder or changed back into a picture by a TV set or picture monitor.

There are two different kinds of pickup devices — the pickup tube and the charge-coupled device, or CCD. A CCD camera is also known as a chip camera because it uses silicon chips instead of tubes in its circuitry.

There are also two types of arrangements for these pickup devices. A one-tube or one-chip camera uses only one pickup device to transform light energy into electronic signals. A three-tube or three-chip camera breaks the light into the three primary colors of light — red, green, and blue. Then, it changes each color into an electronic signal. Three tubes or chips make a sharper television picture than one tube or chip will, so most professional videographers (people who earn money by making videos) use a three-tube or three-chip camera.

The Television Receiver

The television receiver contains a cathode ray tube or CRT. The CRT, also called a picture tube, is made of glass and, like a light bulb, all the air has been removed from the inside to create a vacuum. At the back of the tube is an electron gun. When electricity enters the gun, it gives off charged particles called electrons. The electrons are focused into three separate beams by electrically charged metal plates and aimed at the front of the picture tube through a *shadow mask*. The shadow mask is a metal plate containing approximately two hundred thousand holes through which the electron beams pass. The plate aims the electrons so they strike the correct phosphors on the TV screen.

What are phosphors? The front of the picture tube is covered with hundreds of thousands of red, green, and blue dots arranged in tiny circles, or pixels. The dots are made of a chemical substance called a phosphor, which radiates light when electrons strike it. Each pixel contains one red, one blue, and one green dot. The three colors correspond to the three electron beams.

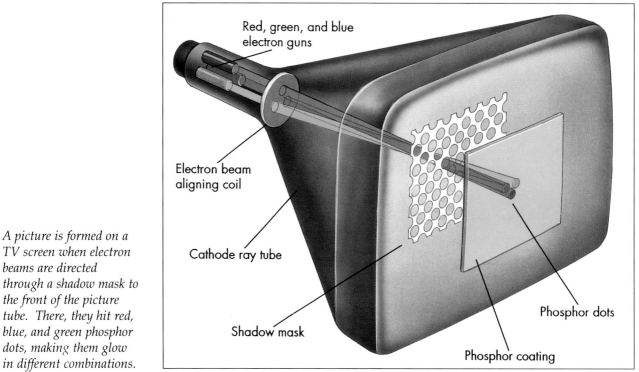

A picture is formed on a TV screen when electron beams are directed through a shadow mask to the front of the picture tube. There, they hit red, blue, and green phosphor dots, making them glow in different combinations.

When an electron beam hits one of the dots, the dot glows, forming one small part of the TV picture. All of the colors in the television picture are created by making combinations of red, green, and blue dots glow at various levels of intensity.

What Happened to Yellow?

You've probably already learned that the three primary colors are red, yellow, and blue. So why are the three primary colors in television red, green, and blue? The answer has to do with how the images are produced.

When you spread red, yellow, and blue paint on a sheet of paper, light waves strike the paper and are reflected back into your eyes. Light is made up of many different waves, each of a different length. Different wavelengths produce different colors.

Colorants or pigments (materials that produce color) absorb some light waves and reflect others, depending on the length of the light wave. For example, when light strikes a splash of red paint, the light with short wavelengths (light that appears blue) and the light with medium wavelengths (yellow) are absorbed by the colorant. But the long wavelength light (the red) is reflected back into your eyes.

Because each colorant absorbs, or subtracts, some of the light that strikes it, the color-producing process is called subtractive color or color by subtraction. You can make any color you want by mixing the three primary colors in different combinations. What you are really doing is mixing colorants that have different rates of absorbing or reflecting light waves.

The process is reversed when color is produced by mixing different colored lights instead of colorants. Here, the light waves are not absorbed by anything. Instead, they are added together. This is called additive color or color by addition. And the primary colors are red, green, and blue. Red and green light mixed together produce yellow; blue and green make blue-green; and blue and red make purple. The three together make white light.

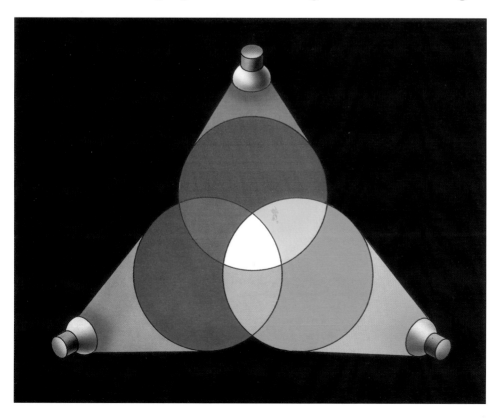

All colors can be produced by mixing the three primary colors of light. When two are mixed in equal quantities, red and green make yellow, blue and green make cyan (blue-green), and blue and red make magenta (purple). If all the primary colors are added together, white light is formed.

Fast Fields Make Moving Pictures

High-definition television (HDTV) cameras on a studio set. HDTV images give a wider picture and are composed of about twice as many scanning lines as ordinary TV pictures. It is hoped that a world standard will be adopted for this new technology. At the moment, different countries use different systems with varying numbers of scanning lines.

The colors change and the television picture moves because of another process called *raster scanning*. Like a movie or a cartoon flip book, a television picture is made up of many separate pictures or frames. These frames appear one after the other so fast that your eye blends them together and you see movement. But unlike movie film, a television frame is made up of two sets of scanning lines, called *fields*.

In the United States, Japan, Canada, and most of South America, television screens contain 525 scanning lines. (This standard system is called the NTSC system, for the National Television System Committee, a group of engineers that developed it.) The electron gun starts at the top and sends beams across every other line from left to right (as you look at the screen)

until it has traced 262.5 lines. Then it goes back up to the top and sends beams across the 262.5 lines that it skipped the first time. The odd scanning lines make up one field, and the even scanning lines make up the other. The two fields together make one frame. And when the TV set is on, the electron gun scans thirty frames per second. That's 15,750 lines every second!

The Videotape Recorder

A videotape recorder (called a videocassette recorder, or VCR, if the tape is enclosed in a cassette) uses plastic or thin metal tape covered with particles that can be magnetized. Most videotape is coated with iron oxide, also called ferric oxide. Some high-quality tape is coated with extremely small particles of pure metal. Metal-particle tape produces a much better recording than iron oxide tape can because the whole particle can be magnetized instead of just the iron part of the molecule.

The videotape recorder, or VTR, records a television signal by taking it off the TV set, a video camera, or another videotape recorder and changing it into an electric current. This current passes through wire coils inside the VTR and then into electromagnets called *recording heads*.

A recording head is a ring of metal with a gap in it. In really good VTRs, the head gap can be as small as three-tenths of a micron (a micron is a millionth of a meter). The electric current creates a magnetic field in the head and over the gap. When the tape passes over the gap, the particles on the tape are magnetized into patterns in the same way that you can create patterns by holding a magnet under a sheet of paper covered with iron filings. These patterns hold the information that makes up the video picture and sound.

The recording heads are mounted on a drum that can rotate thirty times every second. This allows the tape itself to move more slowly (*see* Chapter 1). The magnetic patterns are laid on the videotape in angled stripes called *tracks*. This is called *helical scanning.* Head A begins its track at the same instant that Head B finishes a track, and vice versa. Each head records a total of thirty tracks per second. That means that a VTR with two recording heads records sixty tracks per second.

The wide video track takes up most of the tape. Audio tracks also runs along one edge of the tape, and along the other edge runs a control track that keeps the video images stable so they don't merge into each other on the television screen. The information on the control track is often called *synchronization information*, or sync. The audio, video, and control tracks are recorded by three separate heads.

Some videotape also includes a time code address track. This allows the videotape recorder to identify each video frame in hours, minutes, seconds, and frame number — very handy when you are editing tape.

A videotape recorder picks up signals from a video camera or TV and changes them to electric currents. These pass through a recording head to a videotape. Particles on the tape are magnetized into patterns of information about the picture and sound.

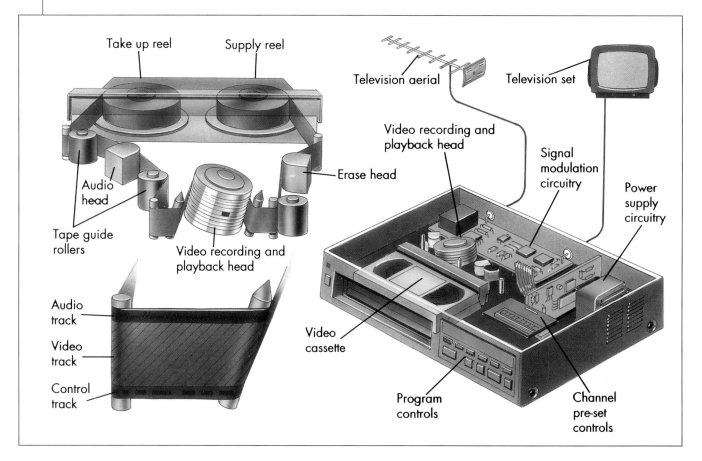

When the videotape is played, the process is reversed. The magnetic impulses on the tape are changed back into electrical current. Then, the current is fed into the television receiver and changed to electron beams in the cathode ray tube.

Notice the relationship between heads, tracks, fields, and frames. Each head in the VTR records one track on the videotape. Each track on the tape corresponds to one field on the TV screen. Therefore, two video heads are needed to record a single frame. The point on the tape where one head stops recording and the second one begins must be timed exactly so that there is no gap or overlap in the tracks, which would be visible in the TV picture.

A batch of new VHS-format video head drums. These sensitive heads are made under dust-free conditions. Millions of bits of information are recorded every second through a tiny gap in the head.

Video Formats

Videotape and videotape recorders come in several formats, some more expensive and of better quality than others. The width of a videotape can range from 8 millimeters (8 mm) all the way up to 2 inches. But most professional broadcasters and videographers use 1/2-inch, 3/4-inch, or 1-inch tape. *Format* refers both to the width of the tape and to the way the tracks are arranged on it.

The tracks on the tape must pass over the corresponding heads in the VTR if the machine is to be able to record on the tape. In the same way, the playback machine must have the same format as the tape; otherwise it won't be able to play it back. The two most common formats for home video recorders are 8 mm and VHS (which uses 1/2-inch tape). (Older home VCRs may also use the Beta format, developed by Sony. Since 1980, however, this format has given way almost entirely to the VHS and 8 mm formats.) Professional broadcasters and videographers often use Super-VHS, Betacam SP, or $3/4$-inch U-matic tape formats. These have features like Dolby noise reduction and enhanced video circuits that make it possible to create many copies or dubs of a tape without losing too much quality.

Analog and Digital Video

The most important recent advance in video has been digital technology. The pixels in analog TV sets are circular. They touch each other, but there is always some black space around the edges, causing the picture to lose resolution, or sharpness and clarity. Also, scattered electronic signals can get into the black spaces and show up as noise, or snow, on the TV screen.

The pixels in digital screens, on the other hand, are square. They fit against each other neatly, with no black space in between, so there is no space for any noise and the resolution improves. You can easily see the difference by comparing the analog picture that your TV set makes with the digital one your computer makes.

Another difference between analog and digital television receivers is in the electron gun. The gun in an analog receiver sends continuous streams of electrons through the shadow mask to the phosphors on the screen. But the gun in a digital set shoots its electrons out in separate pulses. Of course, it does this so fast that your eye sees an unbroken image.

Digital video systems can interface with any other computer-based system. This means that your VCR and your telephone can be connected so that you can call a video "catalog," for example, and order the merchandise you see on your screen through your television set (*see* Chapter 7).

The recording quality of digital video recorders is also a lot better than that of analog systems because the digital signal is not as susceptible to interference or noise as the analog system is. And while analog sound is second-rate at best, digital video systems can provide sound quality equal to that of a compact disk player.

Film or Video?

It's easy to confuse film and video when you're watching it. But they are actually two very different processes, each with its own advantages and disadvantages.

One advantage of video is that it is electronic: Videotape can be recorded and then played back immediately. On the other hand, movie film must be processed, or developed, before it can be viewed. Videotape can also be erased, and a new recording can be made on it right away. But once film has been exposed to light, that's it. To make a new picture, you have to get new film, shoot the new picture, and then develop it.

This makes video a very convenient medium for shooting live action, especially television commercials or shows that broadcast every day, like soap operas. Instead of waiting until the film is developed before they decide which scenes to keep and which scenes to throw away, directors can save a lot of time and money by using video. Videotape provides instant feedback; it allows directors to make artistic decisions immediately.

One more difference: Film has a much higher resolution than video does. However, the new high-definition video cameras and monitors can produce pictures that are as sharp and clear as 35-millimeter film. These cameras are very expensive because the technology is still new. But by the year 2000, many television stations will be broadcasting in the high-definition, or advanced television (ATV), format. And high-definition TVs and VCRs for the home will be on sale.

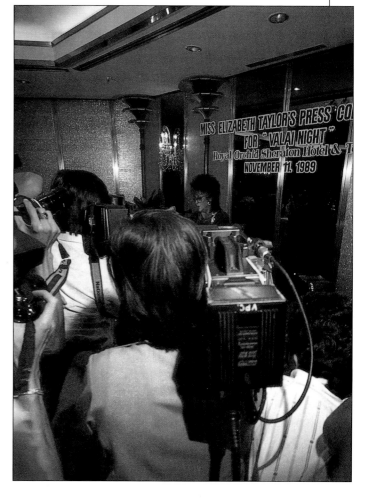

Actress Elizabeth Taylor holds a press conference in Thailand. Video is superior to film when recording news events because it can be played back and edited immediately after recording to meet TV deadlines.

Denise Gallant

Denise Gallant is a video effects designer who also develops special effects equipment. Over the past twenty years, she has created hundreds of special effects for movies, television commercials, and concerts, including extravagant laser light shows for live concerts by the Grateful Dead and Super Tramp.

Gallant was born on February 27, 1951. As a teenager, she wrote and illustrated books for her two younger sisters and spent a lot of time watching her grandfather draw. As he worked, he taught Gallant artistic principles that she would use later in life.

"My grandfather was my inspiration," she says. "His pictures are still in my house on all of my walls."

She also learned from her mother, Beverly Gallant, an actress who worked as an extra for the Hollywood movie studios. As they watched old movies on television, her mother would explain how movies were made. One of Gallant's favorites was Walt Disney's *Fantasia*, which she watched again and again.

In the third grade, Gallant discovered science. Many people tried to discourage her, telling her that she wouldn't be able to succeed in science because she was a girl. But Beverly Gallant told her daughter that there were no limits to what she could do if she worked hard.

In college, Gallant studied film and creative writing. She also learned photography, a skill that helped her later when she began to work in video and multimedia. When she graduated in 1976, she was hired as a video editor for NBC. She was one of two women in a department of ninety men and one of the first women editors at the network.

In the late 1970s, special effects equipment was large and cumbersome, so while she was working at NBC, Gallant and a friend began to design and build video effects machines that were portable and easy to use. They took their new equipment to the Hollywood studios to make music videos and movies or to rock concerts where they produced light shows.

In 1987, Gallant became an advanced systems planner for CMX/Aurora, a video editing and graphics company in California. There, she continued her work, designing equipment to produce ever more complicated and beautiful visual effects. Gallant and her husband also began to create special video effects on CD-ROM for sale to the public. Their first CD-ROM was released in 1994.

Gallant is both an artist and an inventor because she creates the technology with which she expresses her visual ideas. She says most of the inspiration for her special effects comes from dreams; when she dreams of interesting images, she invents the machines to make them. Her latest project is to develop a three-dimensional video recorder. The machine will use laser light to make a 3-D image that, like a hologram, can be viewed without special glasses.

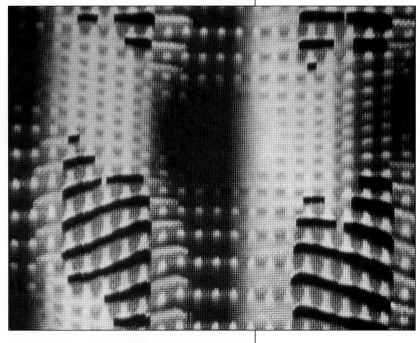

(Above and below) Two examples of Denise Gallant's video art.

Effects Equipment

Some of the most interesting pieces of video equipment are machines that produce special effects like rotating a video image, enlarging or reducing it, blurring it, or changing its colors. One of the most popular machines is called the Video Toaster. Unlike earlier devices, the Video Toaster is relatively inexpensive, which makes it popular with small TV stations or cable companies that can't afford to spend a lot of money for network-style equipment.

The Video Toaster consists of a character generator, special video effects, a three-dimensional (3-D) animation program, and a video paint program that lets you alter or "paint" images on your television screen.

Several good books are available to teach you how to use a video camera and recorders to create your own videos. And it will not be long before someone makes a special effects machine for the home. Then you'll be able to create all kinds of interesting images with your own TV set and VCR. If you want to see how the pros do it, perhaps you can arrange a field trip to a local TV station. Seeing how a real commercial is made or a news show is produced can give you many ideas for your own productions.

Part of a large editing suite. The editors use computer software to manipulate the images on the screens.

Chapter 3
Across the Pacific

While U.S. companies were fiercely competing to build the first videotape recorder, a parallel effort was being made across the Pacific Ocean in Japan. World War II had devastated Japan, but it had also pushed the small country to make hundreds of technological advances.

A young Japanese engineer named Masuru Ibuka thought that all of this new technology should be used to help improve the lives of ordinary people. "'First for consumer' is my idea," Ibuka told one historian.

In 1946, Ibuka formed Tokyo Tsushin Kogyo (the Tokyo Telecommunications Engineering Corporation) — Totsuko for short — with Ako Morita, a young student. The company's mission was to use Japan's highly advanced military research to help the country reconstruct its culture.

In 1947, a twenty-one-year-old mechanical engineer named Nobutoshi Kihara joined Totsuko. His first assignment — to make a small and inexpensive audio recorder that could be used in Japanese homes and schools. Six years later, Kihara began tinkering with the idea of a videotape recorder, but when he found out what Ginsburg and Dolby were doing at Ampex, he stopped. He realized that he couldn't make a videotape recorder that was as good as theirs without copying their ideas. Besides, the Ampex machines were huge models that stood on the floor, and Kihara's company, which had by then changed its name to Sony, still wanted to make products for the general population. Japanese consumers would not be able to buy enormous videotape recorders that cost tens of thousands of dollars.

> **AMAZING FACTS**
>
> Having to design an audio recorder that was gentle enough to use paper tape without breaking it was one of the keys to Kihara's (and Sony's) later success. The recorders had to operate perfectly. The discipline of making such reliable machines was one of the important contributions to the company's success. Even today, Sony is known for the quality of its products.

Nobutoshi Kihara

When Nobutoshi Kihara was growing up in Tokyo, Japan, he liked to read about the new scientific and technological discoveries being made every day in the early twentieth century. Like many Japanese youngsters, he also enjoyed painting and handicrafts, but he was especially interested in, as he says, "the making of clocks and miniature railroads." Kihara also greatly admired the work of the American scientist, Thomas Edison, whose hundreds of inventions inspired the young boy's scientific curiosity even further.

Kihara was born October 15, 1926, in Tokyo. In junior high, he met a teacher who encouraged his interest in science, and he started taking as many science courses as he could fit into his schedule. After earning a degree in mechanical engineering from Waseda University, Kihara went to work for Masuru Ibuka at Totsuko (later known as Sony Corporation). Kihara's first assignment was to develop an audiotape recorder like the German Magnetophon. Later, Ibuka set him to work on a video-tape recorder. Ibuka wanted both machines to be small enough and inexpensive enough so that ordinary people could buy and use them.

All through his career, Kihara strove to make his products smaller. And in achieving this goal, he fulfilled Ibuka's vision of bringing high technology to every home. In 1955, Kihara developed a transistor radio, replacing the cumbersome vacuum tubes with the tiny transistors that Bell Labs in the United States had developed several years earlier. The pocket-sized radios became best-sellers all over the world.

A few years later, Kihara made a transistorized television set that ran on batteries. The smallest had a four-inch (ten-centimeter) screen. It was called "Tummy Television" because you could rest the set on your stomach and watch it while you were lying down.

Kihara generally worked alone when he was developing the prototype products. But when the design was finally correct, he worked together with Sony's manufacturing engineers to make the finished machines. In fact, Kihara says, his department was something like a school. He told one historian, "People come to my school and study new products for one, two, or three years, and then, when the product is finished, they go out into the production side — ten, twenty people at a time."

Throughout his years with Sony, Kihara rose higher and higher in the company, becoming a director in 1970 and senior managing director in 1982. He collected more than seven hundred patents and a number of awards for his work, including the prestigious Medal with the Purple Ribbon from the Japanese Emperor in 1990.

Today, Kihara still works with Sony at a Tokyo research center named after him — the Sony-Kihara Research Center. He is happy with the way video technology has grown because, he says, it "contributes to human happiness and development."

In the future, he thinks video technology will improve even more: "It will have larger capacity, it will be more compact and lower cost." But Kihara believes that the most important contribution of video technology will be to record the history of our world for future generations.

In 1961, Nobutoshi Kihara developed these transistorized TV sets that ran on batteries.

A 1975 Sony videotape recorder. It used the recently developed Betamax 1/2-inch tape. In the 1970s, home recording became popular, and the Betamax system was the first to dominate the market.

Shrinking the Machine

In order to make the devices smaller, Kihara developed the idea of *skip-field recording*. Instead of having the electron gun scan both fields of a frame, it scanned only one field, every other line of the television picture, and then doubled that image. The picture was slightly hazy, but viewers in 1953 were used to interference. The videotape recorder could be made smaller because only half the amount of tape was necessary. In 1959, Sony marketed its first black-and-white skip-field recording VTR.

But, in 1959, color TV was already flooding the market. Skip-field recording couldn't pick up enough signal information to make the colors true to life. Kihara had to find a way to keep the VTR small while making it record all of the lines of the picture.

Finally, in 1969, Kihara and his team of engineers invented the U-matic cassette. In this system, the tape — which is 3/4 inch wide — is automatically pulled from a cassette about the size of a hardcover book by a set of pins mounted on a ring and then wrapped around the head drum in the shape of a sideways U. The U-matic quickly became popular with schools and businesses. But it was very expensive; it still wasn't a machine that every family could use.

Smaller Still!? You've Got to Be Kidding!

Ibuka told Kihara to make a video cassette that was no bigger than a paperback. So Kihara built the first Betamax cassette with tape that was 1/2 inch wide. It used a technique called *azimuth recording* to eliminate the guard band between the tape tracks.

In a U-matic cassette, the video tracks are separated from each other by a space known as a *guard band*, which keeps the signals from one track from interfering with the signals from another. Kihara had been trying to think of a way to eliminate that space so he could make his cassettes smaller. In azimuth recording, the two video recording heads are angled slightly on the tape, one leaning to the left and one to the right. Thus, when the tape is played back, it's much harder for the heads to pick up signals from the wrong track.

Azimuth recording had been used only on black-and-white tape. When Kihara tried it for color videotape, the picture was extremely snowy. But Kihara adjusted the color phase of the tracks and refined the tape transport mechanism to make it gentler. He also made the recording head smaller and changed the magnetic medium on the videotape from iron oxide to a cobalt alloy. The new Betamax 1/2-inch tape could record an hour's worth of video and audio, and it was indeed only the size of a paperback. Ibuka's dream was realized.

The Contributions of Ampex and Sony

A Sony product of the 1990s. Modern video cameras like this one use silicon chips in their circuitry. The screen shows the image in view.

Two pioneer companies, Ampex and Sony, took different directions, Ampex developing the big, high-quality professional machines and Sony the smaller, inexpensive products for the home consumer. Since the 1970s, companies like JVC, Matsushita, Panasonic, and Toshiba have taken these discoveries and improved on them, developing every more versatile and specialized video cameras, recorders, monitors, and supporting equipment. There are more than four hundred companies marketing to the world's video users. Ibuka, Kihara, Poniatoff, Ginsburg, Dolby, and all the others can be proud of their contributions to video technology.

—— Chapter 4 ——
Helping the Police and Businesses

V ideo has exploded into practically every field of human endeavor. It is becoming ever more important to businesses and schools, to scientists and doctors, and to police and other law enforcement officials. Almost three-fourths of all U.S. homes have VCRs, and more than half own a video camera or camcorder.

Law Enforcement and Security

This book began with a fictional scenario in which a miniature video camera concealed inside the brim of a hat was used to record an illegal drug deal. The tiny videotape provided enough evidence for the police to convict the criminals.

The scene may have been fictional, but the miniature cameras are very real. One camera, called a SWATCAM, can record video in total darkness for up to 30 feet (9 meters) by using infrared light. The camera is only $1 3/4$ inches (4.5 centimeters) wide, so it can be inserted into openings as small as two inches (5 centimeters) in diameter. And the lens is mounted on a telescopic probe that can swivel to catch images at any angle. The SWATCAM is an important tool for police sting operations.

Another company makes a microvideo camera only $1 1/2$ inches (3.9 centimeters) square with a pinhole lens only $1/32$ inch (1 millimeter) wide. This camera could have been used in our fictional drug bust, but it is also important in routine police work. The camera and a tiny microphone can be mounted inside a special rear-view mirror in a police squad car and connected to a compact VCR on the dashboard. When a police officer pulls another car over for a traffic offense like speeding, the equipment records the stop. The recording can be used to document what really happened in case there are any questions about the arrest.

Law enforcement officials also use video to train new police officers. Videos teach rookies how to defend themselves in case of an armed attack, how to use their firearms, how to investigate murder cases, and how to interact with the people on their beat.

Video cameras are used in jails and prisons so that inmates can be watched without anyone having to be physically present. The cameras record any movements in the area and send video signals to television monitors (usually TV screens with no sound) in the guardroom, where guards constantly watch them to make sure the prisoners' cells are secure.

Business and Manufacturing

Of course, many businesses also use video cameras for security. Look at the ceilings and walls of your local bank, for example, and you'll see mounted cameras that record the movements of cus-

Video monitors in the security room of a large office block display pictures from video cameras around the building. If staff see anything suspicious, they can control the cameras from a distance.

tomers and bank officers. If there is a robbery, the videotape can be used as evidence in court.

In many businesses, video is used to train new employees in how to handle paperwork, how to sell on the telephone, or how to operate a machine. One soup company uses video to show production workers how each job contributes to the final can of soup. New employees learn how to safely operate various machines by watching videotapes. And

when they have learned their jobs, the workers can make videotapes of themselves operating the machines. Seeing themselves on video helps them improve their skills even more.

Video is especially useful for training people to do dangerous jobs. Railroads set up video cameras in narrow tunnels or on bridges and then use the videotapes to teach workers how to perform their jobs safely. Other companies use video to teach "people" skills, such as the best ways to interview job applicants, to give a speech, or to supervise workers. Trainees can also watch tapes showing them how to handle a stressful situation in the office or with a customer. Then, they can role-play a similar situation, videotape it, play it back, and learn by watching their own performance.

Many companies train their salespeople with videos that show new products and how they will benefit the customer. International companies can save money by using videotapes to train employees instead of sending people on courses. Finally, videos keep employees informed. One national beer company has more than six hundred distributors. Instead of a newsletter, the company sends out a video every month that explains new products to the distributors and shows them how to promote and sell the products.

Students in a business course watch a video showing them how to improve their interview skills. They can learn from prerecorded examples, or their own performance can be recorded and discussed.

Video Also Sells

If you've been out shopping recently, you've probably seen TV screens set up next to a product display. Retail stores use video to explain to customers how products work and what makes them different or better than other, similar products. These "why-buy" videos work especially well for complicated machines like refrigerators, automatic washers, or cars because the video can show the device's interior and explain how it works in a way that most customers will understand. Also, many customers feel more comfortable watching a video than listening to a salesperson.

Hotels and resorts send attractive videos of their grounds and restaurants to travel agents, hoping that the agents will recommend them to their business clients. Real estate companies make videos of homes they have for sale to show prospective buyers.

Teleconferencing

One final way businesses use video is for teleconferencing. Frequently, a company has offices all over the country or the world. It is often inconvenient or too expensive for employees to travel back and forth to meet. Telephone conference calls can help, but because the people in the meeting can't see each other, conference calling isn't ideal.

But teleconferencing allows the participants to be connected via both telephone and video. As they speak to each other on the telephone, a video camera at each location records the meeting. The signal is sent up to a communications satellite and then bounced back down to the other offices where it is received by an antenna and played on a TV set in the meeting room.

These are only a few examples of the many ways that video has changed the way people do their jobs. And the uses of video in the workplace will only continue to increase. As government and industry develop the information superhighway (*see* Chapter 7), more and more people will use video to communicate with each other.

AMAZING FACTS

Business teleconferencing will soon be as common as the telephone. Intel Corporation has designed a small microprocessor that plugs into a desktop computer. A video camera attached to the computer screen creates a video image of the user and transmits it over telephone lines to another computer at another location. Computer users can work on a document at the same time that they see and talk to each other in a window on the computer screen.

Executives in a business teleconference watch a colleague on a video screen.

—— Chapter 5 ——
Video Educates, Trains, and Preserves

If you were a student at Princeton Community High School in Princeton, Indiana, you'd have a different schedule than most high school students do. Besides taking history tests and doing algebra homework, you'd be busy writing scripts for a daily TV magazine show or directing a segment about your school's latest basketball victory. You could even be anchoring a news program. It's all part of running the high school's community TV station, which broadcasts student productions for the whole town to enjoy.

Every week, the students have different jobs to do. They run the cameras, anchor the programs, direct the productions, and sometimes they do the postproduction editing and special effects. In the process, they're learning how to use a lot of equipment that most students never even get a chance to see, and many have gone on to earn college degrees in television and video.

To raise money for the station, the students produce videos for the town's businesses. For example, they made a promotional video for a clock company that explained how clocks are manufactured. Another video, produced for the Princeton Chamber of Commerce, was sent to Japan and Korea to help attract new business from those countries to the Princeton area.

In the Air and on the Road

Midnight at Chicago's O'Hare airport: A jumbo jet carrying 273 weary passengers is preparing to land. Suddenly, the pilot feels a sharp pull to the left. A warning light on the instrument panel tells her that the jet's right engine has lost power. The runway lights jitter as the plane shudders and veers away from the landing strip.

Actually, there are no passengers, and the pilot is in no danger. She is sitting in a flight simulator, which is like a powerful video game. In front of her is a fully equipped airplane instrument panel. Just above her head is a bank of video screens where the cockpit windows would normally be. The simulator sits on hydraulic legs that can pitch and turn the cockpit so the

The cockpit of a flight simulator imitates a Boeing 737 landing at dusk. Simulators can imitate many emergencies and re-create the layouts and conditions of many major airports.

A student uses an interactive video program to study the Russian language. With interactive video, students can each learn at their own speed; this makes for a more flexible learning experience than provided in a classroom.

student pilot feels movement as if she were in a real airplane. The video screens are fed pictures by a powerful computer that can simulate any possible weather condition or mechanical emergency as well as duplicate the runways of almost any airport.

The flight simulator seems so real that the student pilot almost believes she is flying a real jumbo jet. But she is safe on the ground, and the instructor sitting behind her can give her immediate feedback on how well she handled the crisis.

Most schools also use video as a classroom teaching tool. But one of the most popular video tools teaches students how to drive. A video camera mounted in the car behind an experienced driver records the movements he uses to handle tight curves in the road, slippery pavement, or in an emergency. During postproduction, this video is combined with shots of the vehicle and the tires, so student drivers can easily see exactly what to do in a dangerous situation before they practice in a real car.

Sports Videos Help Athletes

Sports trainers also use video as a teaching tool. Weight lifters, gymnasts, ice skaters, tennis stars, football players, and many other athletes use videos to improve their form and avoid dangerous mistakes. By watching a video of an expert gymnast, for example, young athletes can learn how to perform a difficult tumbling routine properly and safely. Their coaches can also record the student routines on video and then play the tape back, pointing out correct and incorrect form.

Teams use video recordings of their plays to help improve their game. Football, basketball, hockey, and many other team sports players can learn to do their own jobs better if they can see the action from several angles, not just from their own positions. This is why you need two or three cameras to videotape team sports — usually one camera up high to get an overview picture, another camera at the end of the playing field, and a third camera operated by a roving cameraperson who can get close-up shots of the players and their moves.

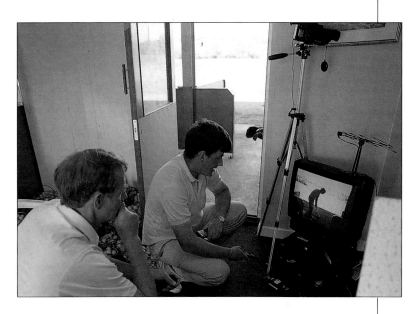

Golfers have their play recorded by a video camera and then watch the tape to analyze their technique and correct any faults they see.

Social Change Through Video

People in underdeveloped countries can use video to improve their lives. In India, most of the people are poor, illiterate, and isolated; they have very little opportunity for education or to lift themselves out of crushing poverty.

In one village, the landlords had illegally taken over most of the village's commonly owned farming land, leaving the poor to starve. So a group of Canadian volunteers set up video equipment under a tree and began playing popular Indian songs on a monitor. When a crowd had gathered, the Canadians started a discussion about the land question. The villagers lost their shyness and told the cameras what it was like not to have enough land to live on while the rich landlords had so much they couldn't farm it all. When the tape was played for the landlords, they made many excuses but refused to part with their illegal holdings. The village council was powerless to force them. So the poor resolved to organize themselves and elect a new village council that could enforce the common land laws.

Orbis is an organization that flies specialist medical staff to underdeveloped countries to perform operations using expensive equipment on people who would normally never have access to such treatment. The operations are recorded on video and relayed to monitors on the Orbis plane to local medical staff who can watch and learn from what they see.

Video can also help people overcome communication barriers. In some countries, it is still customary for women to keep silent in the presence of men. One drought-prone village built a new dam, making water available for the first time. A village meeting was held to determine how the water should be shared. But the women, who would be the main users of the water, were not consulted, and they refused to speak in front of the men. So a video was made in which the women were able to present their views, and the tape was later played back at a meeting of the men. After seeing the tape, the men were able to plan for the women's water needs as well as their own.

Recording Today for Future Generations

Educators and other trainers are using video more because many people learn better by seeing and hearing about something than by simply reading about it. While there will never be a substitute for the written word when it comes to presenting ideas, many physical objects and events can be understood more easily through pictures. That's why historians are excited about the possibilities video offers for recording and preserving the events and images of the world around us for future generations to study.

On the Flathead Reservation in Montana, only a few elderly Native Americans still speak their native Salish language. And because Salish has never been a written language, there is no way to preserve it after these last speakers die. But preserving the

Salish language and history is important, especially for the young people who want to understand the traditions of their ancestors.

So a community television station at Salish Kootenai College on the reservation is producing video recordings of the elders as they tell stories about the tribe's history. The videos also document ancient hunting and fishing sites and show how the tribe's artisans make traditional tools and clothing decorated with quills and beads. These carefully produced videotapes preserve not only the history of the people but the language itself for future generations to study and cherish.

Ordinary people, too, use video instead of still cameras to preserve the images and sounds of their children as they grow up or to record family celebrations to be enjoyed again and again. In Ethridge, Tennessee, a small town of only eight hundred people, an energetic grandmother named Sarah Evetts operates a small television station just for the people of Ethridge. The transmitter in her back yard broadcasts birthday parties, church gatherings, family reunions, and high school football games. If the people of Ethridge want Evetts to air a party or a game, all they have to do is telephone, and she'll come over with her camcorder, make a videotape, and take it back to the VCR in her basement where she plays it for the whole town. Someday, historians will be able to use her videos to see what life was like in Ethridge at the end of the twentieth century.

As you can see from the examples in this chapter, video is not just a tool for professionals. With modern equipment — easy to use and inexpensive — anyone can produce video for almost any purpose. In fact, the possibilities are limited only by your imagination.

AMAZING FACTS

Sony's Betacam tape has been the most popular format for schools, sports videographers, and other professionals ever since it was introduced in 1982. Since then, Sony has sold more than 100 million Betacam cassettes worldwide. If all those cassettes were placed end to end, they would span the entire United States, east to west, three times. They represent almost three thousand years of recording.

In many homes, camcorders are used to record all the important events of family life.

Chapter 6
Video for Science and Art

A scientist uses a light microscope and video monitor to examine white blood cell lines of families who suffer from inherited diseases. Such studies are beginning to discover which human genes are responsible for which inherited diseases.

Modern technology can do amazing things with a video image. A picture that appears to be nothing but noise can be manipulated until an image appears. Images hidden in fog can be sharpened. Objects can be measured, counted, sorted, and played back in slow-motion or high-speed or looked at individually in freeze frames. Sound can be dubbed in. And all of this can be done with pictures taken with everything from an electron microscope to a radio telescope or satellite radar.

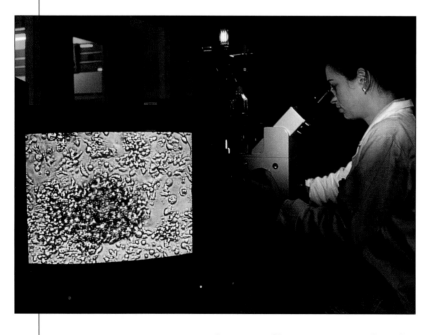

Atoms to Galaxies

One example is video microscopy, in which video and computers are used to enhance objects seen through light microscopes, the kind of microscope probably found in your school's science lab. The image under the microscope can be viewed on a television set so that many people can see it at the same time. It can also be electronically manipulated to make it clearer. Contrasts can be sharpened, and ultraviolet and infrared light (ordinarily invisible to human eyes) can be made visible.

The same technique is used in medicine. In a procedure called endoscopy, doctors can insert an endoscope, a flexible fiber optic tube, into a damaged artery or organ. The fiber optic tube is connected to a video camera outside the body, and the image is displayed on a video monitor. Surgeons can actually perform some operations simply by inserting an endoscope and laser-powered surgical instruments into a body opening like the mouth or through a tiny incision in the skin. The surgical team performs the surgery by watching the process going on inside the body on the monitor. This procedure is much safer than traditional surgical methods because the small incision reduces the chance of infection, and patients heal faster and with much less pain.

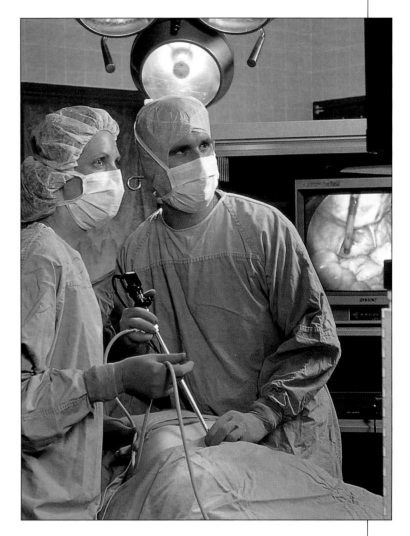

Surgeons insert a tube containing optical fibers into a patient's abdomen. This tube is connected to a video camera, and the image it produces is displayed on the video monitor. The process enables surgeons to perform an operation on an area they could only otherwise see by using drastic and tissue-damaging surgery.

Even dentists find video useful. They can insert a tiny video camera into a patient's mouth to see teeth from all angles. Then, they can manipulate the enlarged picture on a video monitor to help them locate and treat tooth decay and disease.

Video also helps explore space. The National Aeronautics and Space Administration (NASA) has shown the world startlingly beautiful video images of our neighboring planets and their satellites, as well as of our own planet. Seeing our blue globe in the blackness of space has made many people realize how fragile it is and how careful we must be to preserve our environment.

Radar images taken from satellites orbiting Earth can be enhanced and interpreted with video. For example, in 1994,

A false-color computer enhancement of the Great Red Spot on the planet Jupiter and the cloud formations around it. The video image has been manipulated to emphasize red and blue at the expense of green.

AMAZING FACTS

In 1622, the Spanish galleon *Atocha* sank, loaded with treasure, off the coast of Key West, Florida. When divers discovered the ship in the early 1980s, they found a cannon that had been sealed with molten iron. Spanish explorers often hid their greatest treasures inside their ships' cannons to keep them safe from pirates. But forcing them open would have destroyed the ancient guns. So, archaeologists inserted a fiber optic tube, connected to a video camera, into a small hole at one end of the sealed cannon. Inside were priceless jewels and ancient ingots of pure gold.

radar aboard the space shuttle *Endeavour* was aimed at the mist-shrouded volcanoes in Rwanda, Zaire, and Uganda, where the world's last remaining mountain gorillas live. The three-dimensional (3-D) radar images of the gorillas' habitat will be enhanced with video and then combined with images gathered from military satellites that show such details as bamboo thickets, nettle patches, and the gorillas themselves roaming the volcanoes. The final pictures will be used to determine where the gorillas live and where they travel — information that is crucial if we are to save this endangered species.

Under the Sea

Space is not the only place that ordinary people can visit through the lens of a video camera. In September 1985, a French and American team of scientists stunned the world by announcing they had found the wreckage of the *Titanic* at the bottom of the sea 350 miles (560 kilometers) southeast of Newfoundland, Canada. Even without cargo or passengers, the ship weighed almost 25,000 tons (22,750 metric tons) and was nearly one-sixth of a mile (one-quarter of a kilometer) long. The *Titanic* was "unsinkable," or so everyone thought.

But on her maiden voyage from England to New York City, she struck an iceberg on her starboard bow. It was 11:40 P.M., April 14, 1912. Three hours later she sank, and 1,522 people drowned. Only 705 survived.

In 1985, French and American scientists formed a mission to find the lost *Titanic*. Using sonar and satellite signals, they were able to narrow their search to a small area, but sonar alone was not enough to distinguish the wreck from the natural formations on the ocean floor. So they launched the *Argo*, an unpiloted submersible craft loaded with video cameras and towed along the ocean bottom 2.5 miles (4 kilometers) below the surface. On September 1, 1985, the cameras on the *Argo* homed in on the *Titanic*'s boiler, sending up video images to the monitors aboard the mother ship.

In 1986, the American scientists returned, this time with *Alvin*, a piloted minisubmarine. Attached to *Alvin*'s underside were two fixed video cameras. A rotating arm thrusting out from the vehicle's front held a still camera and a third video camera. And inside a steel cage bolted to *Alvin*'s bow was a tiny spherical submarine named *Jason Jr.* The little "swimming eyeball," as the team called it, was an underwater robot filled with video equipment.

Alvin was able to capture video pictures of the massive *Titanic*, but only from the outside. *Jason Jr.*, the little swimming eyeball, however, was

AMAZING FACTS

In 1994, the ferry *Estonia* sank off the coast of Finland, killing more than nine hundred people. Diving to the wreckage was too dangerous, so a robot submarine equipped with video cameras was used to find the ship. After examining the video footage, scientists concluded that the ferry had sunk when a storm tore its cargo door off, letting water pour into the hold.

This image of breakfast dishes aboard the Titanic *was taken in 1987 when a small underwater robot with video equipment entered the wrecked ship.*

small enough to enter the wreck and record the ship's grand interior, still hauntingly beautiful after three-quarters of a century at the bottom of the sea.

From Ancient to Avant Garde

Some places, although accessible, could be damaged if large numbers of people were to visit them. In December 1994, archaeologists crawling through a cave in southern France suddenly discovered hundreds of paintings of horses, wooly mammoths and rhinoceroses, bison, panthers, owls, and other wild animals. The animals are running, galloping, or even fighting. It is the largest group of cave paintings ever discovered, and some say they are the most beautiful ever found.

But these cave paintings are twenty thousand years old and extremely fragile. If they are opened to the public — and the outside environment — sooner or later they will flake off the cave walls because of the constant changes in temperature and humidity. To avoid this, the French government plans to record

AMAZING FACTS

The oldest body on Earth was discovered in 1991 in the Tyrolean Alps. The Ice Man lived about four thousand years ago and probably died in a blizzard or an avalanche. His body was so well protected by the snow and ice that it was still in excellent condition when it was found. With it were nearly perfectly preserved shoes, clothes, and tools. The Ice Man's body should be in a museum for the public to see, but it would quickly disintegrate if it were not kept in a special room with carefully controlled humidity and temperature levels. Instead, scientists are making video recordings of the body and of their research on it, so people all over the world can see it as well.

The four thousand-year-old mummified body found on a glacier in the Tyrolean Alps in 1991. The body is so fragile that it cannot be kept on display in a museum. Instead, scientists are making a video of the body and of their research on it.

the cave paintings on video and show them to the public on television, CD-ROMs, and other multimedia devices.

Video has become so important that it was inevitable that someone would begin to see it as more than a tool for viewing our world. While cave paintings are the some of the earliest art ever created by human beings, video art is some of the most recent.

In 1963, the Korean video artist Nam June Paik presented his first exhibition in New York City. Since then, many other artists have begun to use video as a creative medium. Video art involves special effects and computerized enhancements of video pictures, but it is more than that. It is also more than documentaries or fictional theater pieces, even though many of these productions are excellent examples of video.

Video artists use video to make statements about the nature of what is real and what is artificial. Video recordings show events that actually happened in the past, but video artists often show the videotapes they make as a part of a musical concert or theater performance that is happening in the present. In this way, they can make a statement about past, present, and future.

They also can play with the color and movement of the picture by artificially interfering with the TV signal. Some video artists use magnets to distort the video picture in interesting ways. This is possible, of course, because video signals are electromagnetic signals, and they can be affected simply by placing strong magnets on the TV receiver.

Modern video artists use all kinds of video equipment to make video art. They may make a raw videotape with a camcorder and then merge the images with film images or pictures recorded from a TV set. Using computerized editing and special effects equipment, they can manipulate the images they've gathered until they have a final tape of video art. But whether the medium is magnets and electronics or powdered roots and berries such as the cave painters must have used, ancient and modern art have one thing in common — they both express an artist's feelings about the world and the living things in it.

Nam June Paik

In early 1995, the National Museum of American Art in Washington, D.C., acquired its first piece of video art. Nam June Paik's *Technology* comprises twenty-five video monitors in a steel and plywood cabinet shaped like an altar. On the monitors are ever-changing video images from all around the world. *Technology* is one of Paik's series of thirteen video sculptures called *Cathedrals*, each of which explores an important aspect of our civilization.

Born in Seoul, Korea, in 1932, Nam June Paik was the first person to use video as a medium of fine art. He studied music composition in high school and went on to graduate from the University of Tokyo with a degree in music, art history, and aesthetics.

Paik admired the work of many avant-garde (or cutting-edge) composers, especially the American, John Cage. Instead of using traditional orchestral instruments, Cage composed pieces from everyday sounds from things like radios, pots and pans, and "prepared" pianos (pianos altered to make odd sounds). Paik met Cage in 1958, and in the following years, the two performed several concerts together.

In 1961, Paik joined a group of artists in the United States and Europe who rebelled against traditional methods of creating art, literature, and music. During this period, Paik created his first video art. The resulting show occupied several rooms of an art gallery. It consisted of thirteen television sets tuned to various stations, three prepared pianos, and a bunch of noisemakers. During part of the exhibition, one of Paik's friends attacked some of the pianos with an axe. It was Paik's way of stating that the old musical forms were no longer enough to express all of his ideas.

Two years later, Paik met an electronics engineer, Shuya Abe, with whom he later produced much of his video art. The two built Robot K-456 who walked, talked, and defecated beans. They took K-456 to many of their concerts and even out for walks on the streets of New York.

Later in his career, Paik began to experiment with altering video images electronically. One of his works features talk-show host Johnny Carson interviewing a guest. Paik recorded the interview off of his home TV set. Then, he placed a live electrical wire on top of his VCR and replayed the tape. The live wire erased the part of each tape that passed directly under it, so that when the tape is replayed, Johnny Carson is interviewing the guest, but with a recurring blank space. The blank space appears every four seconds at first, but as the tape plays (and gets closer and closer to the core of the tape reel), the blank space appears more and more often.

In other words, the artist literally reached into the TV program and made a mark on it — or several marks! Nan June Paik was saying that TV audiences can — and should — become involved with television instead of just sitting passively and watching. This tape was made in 1966, long before interactive television was even thought of by most people.

Nam June Paik with one of his sculptures, a robot called Satellite Baby. *The robot's body displays TV, cable, and satellite images.*

— Chapter 7 —
A Future of Ultimate Interactions

Until the early 1980s, video was delivered to consumers either through broadcast or via coaxial cable. Broadcast television uses electromagnetic waves to send data and pictures from the television transmitter to the television receiver. Coaxial cable (coax for short) carries electronic signals through cable wire.

Recently, however, a new transmission medium — glass fiber — has been developed and is being rapidly installed by telephone and cable companies around the world. Fiber optic cable is made of strands of glass as thin as a human hair. This glass is so pure that if it were made into a window 70 miles (113 kilometers) thick, you could still see clearly through it. Fiber optic cable can carry 250,000 times as much data as a standard copper telephone wire, making it possible to transmit the contents of the entire *Encyclopedia Britannica* in a single second. Fiber optics have made it possible to begin building the information superhighway, the enormous network of telephone, video, and computer technologies that could eventually connect everyone in the world via computer and modem with each other and with all of the world's libraries, museums, and art galleries.

How Fiber Optics Are Used

Because it can transmit so much more information than copper wire, fiber optic cable makes it possible to interact with your television programs. One example of interactive television is video-on-demand, or VOD. With VOD, you can call up a menu of programs on your TV screen and then select which one you want to see. Imagine being able to watch an episode of "Star Trek" whenever you wanted instead of having to wait until it came on next or having to record it on your VCR first.

Video shopping at an airport terminal. You can order goods for yourself or have them mailed as gifts to friends all over the world.

With video dial tone, television programming is delivered to your home over fiber optic telephone wires instead of coax. If your parents are watching a home shopping program and want a new kitchen gadget, instead of telephoning the program hosts, all they must do is touch a button on the remote control to bring up ordering information on the TV screen. With the remote, they answer questions about the number of items, the color, and the style they want. Then, they simply swipe a credit card through a slot in a box on top of the TV, and in a few days their new gadget arrives in the mail.

People will also be able to pay bills electronically; buy tickets to sports events, concerts, plays, and other entertainment; make reservations with airlines, rental car agencies, and hotels; buy and sell stocks and bonds; and take college courses. Many of these will be videotex (or videotext) services, that is, simple menus arranged on the TV screen in fixed frames, very much like the menus computer software produces. Others, however, will be full multimedia presentations with moving video, sound, and animated graphics.

Playing a video game on a home computer. Today, games can be called up on and played through a TV set if you subscribe to an interactive video game service.

Video and Computers

Of course, many of these services are already available to people who subscribe to the Internet or another on-line communications service over their home computers. On the Internet, for example, you can find anything that's in the Library of Congress or the Smithsonian Institution or call up pictures of the art in the Louvre or of the ancient Roman ruins in Italy. You can download articles on virtually any subject in any language from all over the world. You can "talk" to people in Greece or China in real time by writing messages that are transmitted back and forth virtually instantaneously. You can watch TV documentaries on your computer screen or even listen to symphonies.

Multimedia applications like this will completely change the way schools teach students. Instead of just reading a book on whales, for example, you will be able to view whales swimming, hear whale song, or even use an interactive computer program to dissect a whale electronically and study its anatomy.

Interactive Video Games

Of course, you may already have played video games through your television set. The Sega Channel, an interactive video game cable service was launched late in 1994. It is the first truly interactive cable service in the United States. When you subscribe, you receive a special adapter cartridge that plugs into your Sega Genesis (TM) game system and attaches to the coax in your home. A menu appears on the television screen, allowing you to select a game, which is then downloaded within a minute into the adapter so you can play it. Eventually, you will even be able to play against another viewer.

In Europe, interactive video is even more elaborate. In one game, called "Crazy Soccer," players in different locations control opposing soccer teams by punching the buttons on their telephones. In another, viewers can control "Hugo," an animated character. An actor at the company's studios wears a special masklike helmet that contains optical fibers. When the actor moves his face, the fibers send signals to a computer that controls the animated character, making it smile or frown — whatever the actor does. Viewers can call the studio and, using the buttons on their telephones, create their own cartoons by controlling more than 250 electronic devices, including special effects like fireworks, stage smoke, or moving electronic chairs.

A sophisticated video game using virtual reality. The monitor displays a virtual environment that the player can enter using a headset and data glove. These send information to the computer about the player's position and movements. The headset projects changing video images of the room into the player's eyes.

The Ultimate Interaction

In Chapter 5, you read how jet pilots are trained in a flight simulator. The simulator moved just like a real airplane, and the bank of video screens in front of the pilot showed computer-generated images of real airport runways. But what if the simulator could make the experience even more real? What if a medical student could learn how to perform an appendectomy, not just by watching but by actually doing the surgery on a "virtual" patient? What if an architect could walk through a house that hadn't even been built yet just to see if the doors are in the best places or the cupboard handles are at a convenient level? What if, instead of just watching a movie, you could be in it? This is what virtual reality is all about.

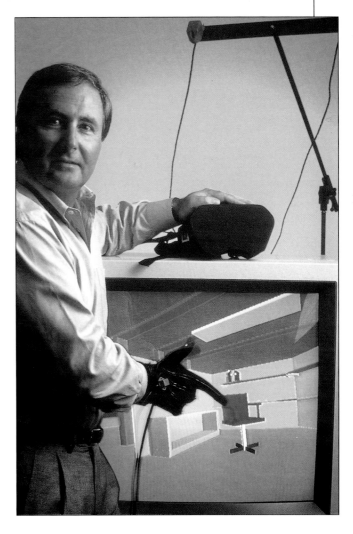

Stanley B. Thomas, Jr. (1942–1995)

When Stanley B. Thomas, Jr., told his thirteen-year-old son about his new job as president of the Sega Channel, the teenager's response was, "Cool! Now you have a real job, Dad!"

Thomas was responsible for launching the first interactive video game channel in the United States and making it succeed as a business. "As a businessman, I know that making a product popular with kids is extremely difficult," said Thomas, "but kids think a video game channel is the ultimate thrill."

When they first started thinking about starting a video game channel, Thomas and other Sega executives gathered groups of kids from all over the country and asked them what they thought the

channel should be like. The children said they wanted great games, previews of new games, contests, and supersecret tips for playing the games. So that's exactly what Thomas gave them. The new Sega Channel became so popular that before it was six months old, cable systems were bringing it to nearly half of the cable homes in the country.

Thomas was born on April 28, 1942 in New York City and was joined by his adopted sister, Jan, eleven years later. Their mother was a homemaker, and their father was a police lieutenant who became a lawyer when Thomas was in his teens. Thomas says he admired his parents a great deal. "My father gave me a sense of values and discipline, and my mother taught me how important all people are."

When Thomas graduated from Yale University, he went to work as an assistant to John Lindsay who was then the mayor of New York City. Then, he went to Washington, D.C., where he eventually became assistant secretary of the U.S. Department of Health, Education, and Welfare.

But after eight years in Washington, Thomas decided to enter the business world. He was especially interested in entertainment, so he joined the rising cable channel, Home Box Office, or HBO. That job led to a series of promotions culminating in the senior vice presidency of Time-Warner Enterprises, where Thomas was responsible for launching several cable channels, including Court TV and New York 1, a twenty-four-hour local news channel. He was so successful that the company asked him to design and lead a new interactive video game channel it was developing with the video game company, Sega of America. When the Sega Channel was incorporated in 1993, Thomas became its president and chief executive officer.

Thomas liked working in television, and he was excited about the new businesses and careers that interactive video is making possible. Of course he also liked video games. "All games are stories, and that's why they're attractive. But it's not just a kids' business. Forty percent of Sega game players are over eighteen." In fact, he said, many players are in their sixties and seventies!

Thomas, too, played a lot of video games with his son. "My son beats the pants off of me," he said. "I think he kind of enjoys it!"

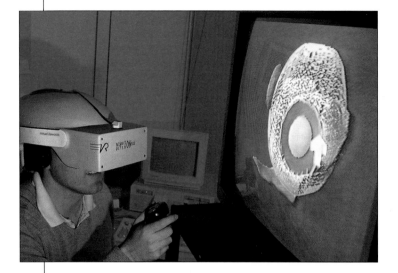

There is no need for a live patient when you can practise eye surgery using virtual reality. You can also see the operation from any angle, unlike with a real patient where views are limited.

AMAZING FACTS

Virtual reality is already being used in retail sales. Shoppers in Tokyo can slip into virtual reality gloves and goggles and enter a virtual kitchen created from their own ideas or from standard designs fed into the computer system. They can run virtual water, open the virtual refrigerator, or even redesign the whole set up on the spot. Then, if they wish to order, the system produces actual plans for the kitchen, plus a contract, prices included.

In essence, virtual reality is a technology that involves the sense of touch as well as sight and hearing. The user wears a helmet that covers the eyes and ears. A tiny screen inside the helmet projects images, and sounds come from the helmet's headphones. The user also wears gloves, or even a whole suit, equipped with flexible fiber optic strands strung along each joint of the hand or body. The fiber optics sense changes in the movement or position of the body and relay them to a computer that makes the virtual environment respond to the movements.

Also in the glove and body suit is a magnetic tracking system that determines the spatial coordinates of the body's position, that is, where it is in relation to the imaginary environment. Wiggle your fingers and the fingers on the video screen inside your helmet wiggle too. Move your leg and the video leg also moves. You can "touch" objects in the virtual environment and even move them around.

Some virtual environments will even include smells. More than thirty basic smells have been identified, and combining these creates hundreds more. Artificial smells are already used in aroma therapy, a psychological treatment technique that uses odors to generate emotional responses and memories. Simply adapting the equipment used in this therapy to the virtual reality helmet will make it possible not only to see, hear, and feel the virtual environment, but also to smell it. Someday you may even be able to taste virtual food!

Visit Mars? Why Not?

NASA scientists are now thinking about using virtual reality to explore planets and galaxies. Really visiting Mars, for example, would be expensive, not to mention extremely dangerous, even for a trained astronaut. But we can send robot craft equipped with video cameras to Mars to gather pictures of the surface. Then, these video images can be manipulated electronically until a 3-D virtual environment is formed. Without leaving Earth, explorers will be able to walk on the surface of our neighboring planet and study it just as if they were actually there.

Virtual reality is not perfected yet, but in time, it may make communication more complete than ever before. Perhaps the technology of the twenty-first century — which started so long ago with Marconi, Farnsworth, and Zworykin — will eventually help all of us learn more about each other and the world we live in.

A multipurpose simulator system allows designers to test many kinds of simulation software including training for hazardous environments such as the oil rig seen here. The wrap-around video display screen fills the users' vision, so they feel immersed in the simulated environment.

Timeline

1931 — I. G. Farben, a German firm, develops coated magnetic tape.

1935 — Plastic audiotape is developed for use in the German Magnetophon.

1945 — Jack Mullin finds Magnetophons in Germany and sends them secretly to the United States.

1947 — Audiotape recorder is developed by several U.S. manufacturers.

1951 — Sony markets the first portable audiotape recorder.

1953 — RCA demonstrates the Simplex video recorder.

1956 — Ampex demonstrates the first broadcast-quality videotape recorder, the Mark IV, at a meeting of CBS affiliates in Chicago. CBS uses videotape to delay broadcast a news program for the first time in history.

1958 — Shiro Okamura develops azimuth recording.

1959 — Sony markets the first compact black-and-white VTR using skip-field recording.

1961 — RCA introduces the TR-22, the first fully transistorized videotape recorder.

1963 — First showing of video art in New York City by Nam June Paik. Birth of video art as a medium of fine art.

1965 — Sony markets a transistorized VTR for home use.

1971 — A committee of representatives from U.S. electronics companies adopts a standard system for videotape, which allows users to play one manufacturer's tape on another manufacturer's machine.

1975 — Sony introduces the Betamax home videocassette recorder. JVC introduces the VHS home VCR.

1977 — First digital videotape recorder is demonstrated in England.

1981 — Sony and Matsushita introduce compact camera/VTR units in Betamax and VHS formats. The age of electronic newsgathering is born.

1994 — Sharp Electronics introduces the Viewcam teleport, the first device able to transmit still video pictures over standard telephone lines. Sega Channel launches the first interactive video game cable service.

Further Reading

Jones, Eurfron Gwynne. *Television Magic*. New York: Marshall Cavendish and Viking Press, 1978.

Lambert, Mark. *TV and Video Technology*. New York: Franklin Watts, 1990.

Larijani, L. Casey. *The Virtual Reality Primer*. New York: McGraw-Hill, 1994.

LeBaron, John, and Philip Miller. *Portable Video: A Production Guide for Young People*. Englewood Cliffs, NJ: Prentice-Hall, 1982.

Meigs, James B., and Jennifer Stern. *Make Your Own Music Video*. New York: Franklin Watts, 1986.

Potter, Tony. *How Television Works*. London, England: Parkwest Publications, 1992.

Renowden, Gareth. *Video: The Inside Story*. New York: Gloucester Press, 1983.

Shachtman, Tom, and Harriet Shelare. *Video Power: A Complete Guide to Writing, Planning, and Shooting Videos*. New York: Henry Holt, 1988.

Glossary

Azimuth recording: A recording process in which the video tracks are set at angles to one another.

Cathode ray tube (CRT): A glass vacuum tube in which electrons are produced and passed through an electric field in the form of a beam to create an image on a phosphor-coated screen.

Control track: The portion of the videotape on which synchronization information is recorded. Keeps the audio and video signals together during playback.

Field: One half of the television picture; one complete vertical scan by the electron gun, of 262.5 lines. Two interlaced fields comprise a frame.

Frame: A complete television picture of 525 scanning lines.

Helical scanning: A video recording process in which signal information is laid on the videotape in angled stripes.

Metal particle tape: Videotape coated with pure instead of oxidized metal.

Noise: Static or interference visible as "snow" or streaks in a video picture.

Phosphors: Chemicals that give off light when they are struck by electrons.

Pixel: A tiny circle (analog systems) or square (digital systems) on the television screen that contains one red, one green, and one blue phosphor dot.

Quadrascanning: Scanning from the center outward. The scanning method used by computer monitors.

Raster scanning: Scanning every other line from the top down. The method of scanning used by television receivers.

Shadow mask: A metal plate in a color television receiver with holes through which electrons pass from the electron gun to the phosphor screen.

Video dial tone: A technology in which video signals are transmitted over ordinary telephone wire.

Video on demand (VOD): A new technology that allows viewers to select video programming "on demand" from a menu.

Videotex (or videotext): An interactive television program comprising only words and numbers. Viewers communicate with the program by pressing buttons on the screen to answer simple questions.

Index

Numbers in *italic* indicate pictures; numbers in **bold** indicate biographies